Detox: Becoming the Best Version of You!

(Reclaiming control of your mental, emotional and spiritual health)

Your Journaling Guide" - Mattathias Johnson

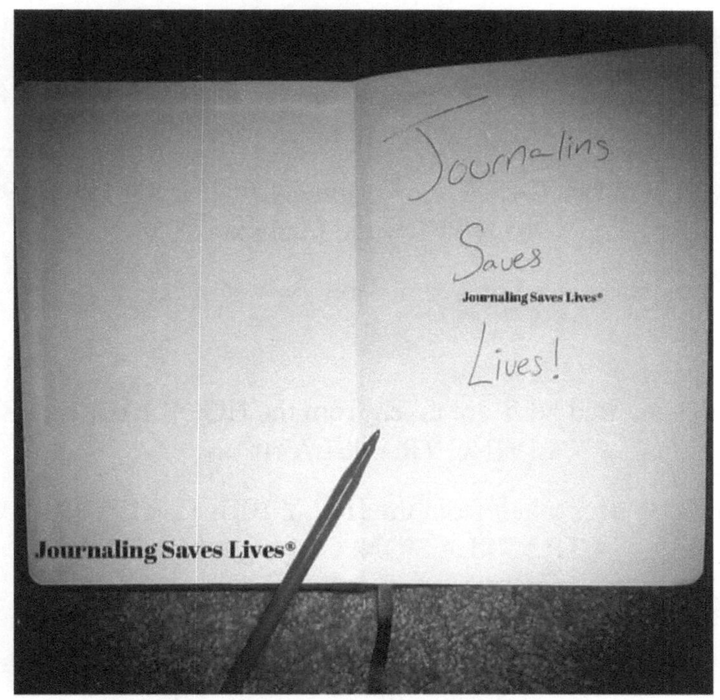

Amazon License Notes

While every effort has been made to ensure the accuracy and legitimacy of the references, referrals, and links (collectively "Links") presented in this eBook, [Author] is not responsible or liable for broken Links or missing or fallacious information at the Links. Any Links in this eBook to a specific product, process, website, or service do not constitute or imply an endorsement by [Mattathias Johnson] of same, or its producer or provider. The views and opinions contained at any Links do not necessarily express or reflect those of [Mattathias Johnson].

Introduction

Journaling Saves Lives is a movement that was started in 2016 that seeks to highlight the importance of being proactive in cultivating and maintaining spiritual, emotional & mental health; by utilizing a simple tool such as journaling to have a release from "inner baggage" brought on by pain, trauma, sorrow, hurt, anger etc... Internalizing the cares of life is dangerous and will cause mental/nervous breakdown, anxiety and other disorders when left unchecked/untreated. Being reactive is a threat to spiritual, emotional & mental health, however being proactive and combating potential issues before it becomes a problem is very key. This is where my movement comes in, we seek to prevent people from going over into emotional distress & mental health decline (onset of mental illness).
We're a "Preventative" Movement!!
Our tagline is: Becoming the best version of YOU!

Background of the Author: Mattathias Johnson, is a graduate of Malone University with a B.A. in business administration along with six sigma certification (process improvement); he's also a 10 year employee of Cleveland Clinic with 8 years of training, coursework and experience in Harassment Prevention, Obesity Sensitivity, Emotional Intelligence & Competence, Diversity & Inclusion, S.T.A.R.T. (a training that teaches active listening, rapport and relationship building) and H.E.A.R.T. (which is a communication system that builds trust, teaches empathy principles between the speaker & listener in all contexts & facets of life).

Foundational Scripture: *Hebrews 12:1 (Amp) "...stripping off every unnecessary weight..."*

The reason I selected this scripture as the foundational scripture for this movement is because upon reading it, I noticed the word "weight" preceded the word "sin." While weights can be the result of sin on the part of the person affected, this is not always the case. There may be areas of our life that are barren and stagnant due to us internalizing anger, hurt, frustration etc. which are things that weigh us down internally. The amplified version of that particular really highlights the effort that we must put forth in our own healing and wholeness.

This book was birthed so you wouldn't have to suffer in silence!

Dedication

This book is dedicated to everyone who's currently taking or planning to take a powerful step towards reclaiming control of their mental, emotional and spiritual health. Often times, the troubles of life place a never ending wear and tear on our inner being. The bigger problem lies in the fact, many people choose to "internalize" rather than cultivating healthy coping mechanisms and effective release methods for this stress. It is my prayer and hope that this book equips people with simple tools and principles but more importantly, challenges them to become the best version of themselves.

2 Kings 5:10-11 (ESV)

10) "And Elisha sent a messenger to him, saying, "Go and wash in the Jordan seven times, and your flesh shall be restored, and you shall be clean." 11) But Naaman was angry and went away, saying, "Behold, I thought that he would surely come out to me and stand and call upon the name of the LORD his God, and wave his hand over the place and cure the leper."

Many people often look for help in long, drawn out or through illustrious methods; however, the most effective help usually comes in those simple ways which forces people to take an active role in their own breakthrough. That is precisely what this book seeks to accomplish. Comprised of Journaling Exercises, memory scriptures, devotional challenges and meditation points you're sure to be set on the path of Soul Healing and Wholeness.

Deuteronomy 1:2 (ESV)

"It is eleven days' journey from Horeb by the way of Mount Seir to Kadesh-barnea."

For the Children of Israel, the 11 day journey to the promise land ended up taking 40 years due to complaining, lack of trust in God and laziness on their part. Unfortunately, because of this, a whole generation died at the judgment of God. This book is symbolically set up according to this passage of scripture; it will serve you well as you journey towards your personal land of Canaan (sound mental, emotional and spiritual health). Warning, don't allow the same hindrances to destroy you as it did the Children of Israel.

Mental Illness

The Numbers!

Approx. 1 out of 5 adults in the USA—43.8 mill. Or 18.5%—experiences mental illness in a given year.

Approx. 1 out of 25 adults in the USA—9.8 mill. Or 4.0%—experiences a severe mental illness in a given year that substantially interferes with or limits one or more major life activities.

Approx. 1 out of 5 youth aged 13–18 (21.4%) experiences a severe mental disorder at some point during their life. For children aged 8–15, the estimate is 13%.

1.1% of adults in the USA live with schizophrenia.

2.6% of adults in the USA live with bipolar disorder.

6.9% of adults in the USA—16 mill.—had at least one major depressive episode in the past year.

18.1% of adults in the USA experienced an anxiety disorder such as posttraumatic stress disorder, obsessive-compulsive disorder and specific phobias.

Among the 20.2 mill. Adults in the USA who experienced a substance use disorder, 50.5%—10.2 mill. Adults—had a simultaneous mental illness.

Social Factors!

An estimated 26% of homeless adults staying in shelters live with severe mental illness and an estimated 46% live with severe mental illness and/or substance use disorders.

Approx. 20% of state prisoners and 21% of local jail prisoners have a previous mental health condition.

70% of youth in juvenile justice systems have at least one mental health condition and at least 20% live with a severe mental illness.

Only 41% of adults in the USA with a mental health condition received mental health services in the past year. Among adults with a severe mental illness, 62.9% received mental health services in the past year.

Just over 1/2 (50.6%) of children aged 8-15 received mental health services in the previous year.

African Americans and Hispanic Americans each use mental health services at about 1/2 the rate of Caucasian Americans and Asian Americans at about 1/3 the rate.

1/2 of all chronic mental illness begins by age 14; 3/4 by age 24. Despite effective treatment, there are long delays—sometimes decades—between the first appearance of symptoms and when people get help.

The Result!

Severe mental illness costs America roughly $193.2 billion in lost earnings per year.

Mood disorders, including major depression, dysthymic disorder and bipolar disorder, are the third most common cause of hospitalization in the USA for both youth and adults aged 18–44.

People living with severe mental illness face an increased risk of having chronic medical conditions. Adults in the USA living with severe mental illness die on average 25 years earlier than others, largely due to treatable medical conditions.

Over 1/3 (37%) of students with a mental health condition age 14–21 and older who are served by special education drop out—the highest dropout rate of any disability group.

Suicide is the 10th leading cause of death in the USA, and the 3rd leading cause of death for people aged 10–14 and the 2nd leading cause of death for people aged 15–24.

More than 90% of children who die by suicide have a mental health condition.

Each day an estimated 18-22 veterans die by suicide.

4 Main Reasons People Internalize Stress

Skepticism: Skeptical means to be negative about things and doubt or disbelieve them. This is a concept that manifests into a lack of trust towards others. Some people feel they're alone and that no one is trust worthy enough for them to share the most intimate or sensitive life matters. Where does this come from? Perhaps from a direct past experience(s) with others that brought about rejection, pain or abandonment. It could also come indirectly, by witnessing others get treated in a negative way which prompts skepticism within one's own self.

Embarrassment: Embarrass means to make uncomfortably self-conscious. People recognize various negative stigmas and discriminations associated with mental illness, emotional distress and the inability to handle stress overall. This then causes fear and shame because people don't want to be labeled "crazy" neither do they want it to appear they have no grip on their life (which may very well be true). They may also have concerns about how this could negatively impact their career, education, or other life goals.

Limited Awareness: People usually dismiss or minimize their issues and say "everyone gets stressed out" or "my problems aren't that bad" or "you're making more out of this than you need to." This is what happens when denial, dismissal or even suppression tarries so long; now the affected either can't see that a problem(s) exist or as mentioned above, they lessen the actual severity.

Dilemma: This one is often overlooked and that is some people are unsure of where to actually go for effective help. Depending on the level of stress people need viable, lasting solutions not just a simple listening ear. The goal is to cure the condition not simply treat the symptoms. In the age of digital mass media, one can almost always find help they need, the question then becomes will they utilize it?

8 Dangers of Internalizing Stress (Physical & Mental ailments that result)

Cardiac: Stress causes the heart rate to speed up at prolonged intervals often resulting in conditions such as tachycardia or irregular heartbeats known as arrhythmias. As blood pressure stays elevated this keeps the heart rate elevated; if left unchecked the more detrimental threat becomes myocardial infarction (heart attack).

Pulmonary: People suffering from high stress tend to breathe heavily and rapidly for long periods of time, putting a heavy strain on their lungs. One then develops a greater risk of panic attacks. During a panic attack, one of the chief symptoms is gasping for air, resulting in hyperventilation.

Gastro: Stress really taxes your gastrointestinal system. When your stomach stays in a state of agitation, there is a greater risk of developing ulcers and IBS (irritable bowel syndrome). Here are some symptoms of a digestive system out of balance: indigestions, acid reflux, constipation, nausea, and diarrhea.

Immune System: Stress places a wear and tear on your immune system. What happens is, in the presence of stress your immune system responds by starting its fighting process as if there is something attacking it. Overtime, it severely weakens then when bacteria or viruses enter the body it leaves your system unable to fight against it.

Depression: It is normal to experience varying or fluctuating moods, in everyday life due to experiences and circumstances. While some "down in the dumps" feelings are a part of life, sometimes, people fall into depressive states that persist and start interfering with their ability to complete major life activities and/or enjoy successful interpersonal relationships.

Anxiety: Some people who are stressed display mild outward signs of anxiety, such as fidgeting, nail biting, constant pacing, etc. In others, a chronic release of stress hormones contributes to more intensive signs of anxiety (e.g., racing heartbeat, nausea, sweaty palms, etc.)

Cognitive Function: Stress hormones often decrease the functioning of brain cells in the hippocampus (a part of the brain that is responsible for short term to long term memory conversion) and in the frontal lobes (the part of the brain that is necessary for problem solving, paying attention and filtering out irrelevant information). As a result, people who are stressed over prolonged periods of time may experience confusion, difficulty concentrating, trouble learning new information, and/or problems with decision-making.

Personality Changes: Some people experience personality changes in response to stress which indeed does alter hormonal levels; and can include irritability, aggression, hostility, obsessive compulsive behavior etc.

What is Journaling?

In my personal opinion, journaling is dumping your personal trash in the trash can. Life is a never ending cycle of events, ideas, stir of information, surprises, frustrations etc…without a proper way to release the mirage of negative emotions, thoughts, and feelings that accumulate in our inner being we are sure headed for death whether literal or symbolically. Journaling may not solve the problem but freeing up mental space will allow you to see the solution or solutions more easily. Journaling is a vehicle to explore emotions, an effective way to channel intense feelings into healthy and productive internal fuel. It is a form of free self-expression that if done properly will always lead to personal growth. By writing down your thoughts and feelings, you are forced to pause from the race of life in order to pay attention to the finest details. You have to listen rather than run away from your feelings.

Disclaimer: In order to thoroughly benefit from journaling, this requires a commitment to 100% honesty & transparency. It's bad to deceive other people but even worst to deceive yourself; in addition, journaling requires consistency in order to maximize benefits. As with anything else, when you're inconsistent, it too will be of little or no value.

What approach should you take in Journaling?

Here are some questions (event/situation focused & general) that will force you to dig deep and make necessary connections as you journal. These questions will allow you deal with the ROOT causes not just the effects; and will make sure you keep a realistic view of what you're dealing with rather than allowing your mind to wonder and create extra yet imaginary stress:

-What happened or what was said, exactly? (Give a realistic account of what happened or what was said).
-When did this occur? (How long ago?)
-If a big amount of time has passed why are you now deciding to deal with/release it?

-Name all parties involved and the specific parts they played? (Include yourself as well)
-What was your initial response when this occurred? (Words & actions)
-What emotions did you display when this happened?
-What were your exact thoughts at the time?
-Has this happened more than once? (If so, what was different this time vs. Prior to?)
-What lessons (positive & negative) can be learned from this experience?
-How do you feel at this very moment (be very specific & detailed)?
-Do you feel loved? (If so, why? if not, why?)
-How do you feel about your life as it stands right now? (Be very specific & detailed)
-Do you consider yourself an emotionally & mentally healthy person? (If so, why? if not, why?)
-Are you content with being yourself or do you feel constant pressure to become someone else?

What are the Benefits of Journaling?

"Journaling helps control your symptoms and improve your mood by helping you prioritize problems, fears, and concerns. Also, tracking any symptoms day-to-day so that you can recognize triggers and learn ways to better control them. Manage anxiety, Reduce stress, Cope with depression. When you have a problem and you're stressed, keeping a journal can help you identify what's causing that stress or anxiety. Then, once you've identified your stressors, you can work on a plan to resolve the problems and, in turn, reduce stress." © 2018 University of Rochester Medical Center – Rochester NY

What does the Bible say?

1 Corinthians 6:19-20 "Or do you not know that your body is a temple of the Holy Spirit within you, whom you have from God? You are not your own, for you were bought with a price. So glorify God in your body."

Many people take this scripture from a one sided aspect as it relates to dealing with sin. The scripture explicitly tells us "we are not our own...so glorify God in our body." Think about it, does God get any glory when we're carrying weight/the cares of life? Those weights & cares actually damage our physical body; so then does a damaged body glorify God? We are defacing something we don't even own, our law would consider this vandalism. When we tear down our bodies we are committing spiritual vandalism which does not bring God glory. Next, let's consider this passage:

Philippians 2:5 "Let this mind be in us which was also in Christ Jesus..."

We can't serve God & Money!
We can't have sweet & salt water coming out of the same fountain!
We can't have the mind of Christ & a mind filled with weights/cares of life. Which tells me that in order to have the mind of Christ I must create space by releasing anything opposed to the mind of Christ. This takes deliberate willpower and a focus aimed at removing these damaging occupants of the mind. The result of winning or losing the battle of the mind goes back to the point of preparation. If you don't train before a battle there is no way you even have a chance to win the battle. What type of preparation/training do we really need in order to win the battle of the mind? Keep in mind that journaling is just one aspect of a healthy lifestyle; to maximize the benefits altogether, here are some other critical areas to include: Adherence to biblical principles in everyday life, consistent prayer & meditation (which is the best time to journal), regular exercise & proper nutrition, healthy friendships & fellowship and fasting (not just from food but rather giving up your favorite activities & other distractions).

Day 1 – **Getting to the Root**

Journaling Exercise #1 (morning):

Hebrews 12:1 (AMP) "Stripping off every unnecessary weight..."
Let's start this day off with a writing method that I call "Purging." Whatever mental, emotional, spiritual debris is left over from yesterday's events and circumstances, take some time to release (you owe it to yourself). It is not a wise idea to drag the cares of yesterday into today; refuse the urge to suppress. You deserve to be free, to experience all of today's hidden blessings. Take 10-15 minutes (or more) for uncensored writing.

Challenge: The more time you allow to elapse without actively putting for effort to gain freedom from sorrow, hurt, anger, trauma etc… the MORE secondary layers (indirectly related problems) begin to cover the core problem(s). This then creates confusion in that, after so long you won't be able to pinpoint the ROOT. And if you can't pinpoint the root, how can you formulate a strategy to overcome? Don't create more internal work for yourself; effectively deal with situations and circumstances in a timely manner.

Meditation point (keep in mind): Unless you have a proper outlet for negative emotions, feelings, thoughts, and ideas there will always be a risk for sporadic or planned outbursts, destructive behavior, self-harming or harming others.

Name 2 points that impacted you the most from Day 1

-

____

____

Day 2 – **The Lie about Time**

Journaling Exercise #2 (morning):

Isaiah 43:18 (KJV) "Remember ye not the former things, neither consider the things of old..."
Often in a subconscious way, we hold onto the cares and troubles of the past. Before your day gets started, take some time (10-15 minutes (or more)) to do some purge writing; release all negative thoughts, fears, worries, concerns, drama, situations, and circumstances. Today will have its own cares therefore, you will need all of your strength for it.

Challenge: TIME DOES NOT HEAL ALL WOUNDS! TIME DOES NOT SOLVE ANYTHING! These are some untruths that have been contributing factors to people remaining locked into pain, heart break, anxiety, anger etc. If you have NOT acknowledged the problem, made the decision to be free and put forth active effort towards the path of healing and wholeness, no matter how much time has elapsed you're still bound. Once again, the danger of letting time pass without actively confronting and dealing with this baggage is, you add more painful layers; suppression and denial gains momentum. Use "Time" to solve your issues NOT deny or become numb to them.

Meditation point (keep in mind): Your physical body will literally break down due to the presence of excess stress hormones. Journaling is a viable option to release that embedded stress.

Name 2 points that impacted you the most from Day 2

____

____

Day 3 – **Attention is a Drug**

Journaling Exercise #3 (bedtime):

Psalm 4:8 (NIV) "In peace, I will lie down and sleep, for you alone, Lord, make me dwell in safety."
How was today; Challenging? Full of adversity? Tumultuous? Angering? Frustrating? Sad? Indifferent? Set aside 10-15 minutes (or more) starting NOW to purge yourself of that negative energy accumulated from today! Consistent journaling, will grant you a new

lease on life because it provides you with a healthy outlet for your emotional baggage and mental tension.

Challenge: Some people DON'T want to be healed and free; in fact, they enjoy being bound and broken (sounds crazy huh?). Why? Because it brings attention and keeps an audience that they may NOT otherwise have. People have literally built their life around this dysfunction; the fact of being "Free" would force them to recreate their entire life. Does this sound like you? Allowing that unhealthy desire for attention will keep you imprisoned to your own pain and will begin to infect those around you. Bring that attention inward.

Meditation point (keep in mind): "You can't pour from an empty cup." Your own mental, spiritual, emotional and physical health is of utmost importance. Let that quote serve as a reminder; self-care first or else you severely restrict your help to others.

Name 2 points that impacted you the most from Day 3

Day 4 – **Walking on the Ledge of Opinions**

Journaling Exercise #4 (morning & bedtime):

Psalm 91:1 (KJV) "He that dwelleth in the secret place of the most high, shall abide under the shadow of the almighty."
Take 10-15 minutes (or more) this morning and before bedtime, to purge; (write down ALL thoughts of fear, distress, worry, anxiety, frustration, sorrow, anger, heart break etc...); remember YOU are the only one who will have access to this journal. This is your day to be

FREE! **Warning:** Keep your journal in a safe place that cannot be accessed by anyone but you.

Challenge: How can you get rid of your "Soul Baggage;" how can you bring stability to your mind, emotions and spirit when you persist on rehearsing and communicating your problems to multiple people? When you do this, a "wise" solution becomes nonexistent because you've opened yourself up to conflicting opinions; about what you should do, what you should say, where you should go etc. which then leaves you unable to decipher the best course of action. Don't let your mouth keep you confined to the very thing(s) you're seeking to be liberated from.

Meditation point (keep in mind): A main reason many people can't get healed, whole and FREE is because they refuse to acknowledge what they are dealing with. Admitting there's a problem and what that problem is, is the first step everyone must take in order to solve it.

Name 2 points that impacted you the most from Day 4

____

____

Day 5 – **The Cost of Manipulation**

Journaling Exercise #5 (bedtime):

Isaiah 40:31 (ESV) "...they who wait for the Lord shall renew their strength..."
Reminder: never take the weights (negative emotions) of the day to bed with you. For the next 10-15 minutes (or more), purge! After you're done, share with us how you feel (leave a comment/post in the

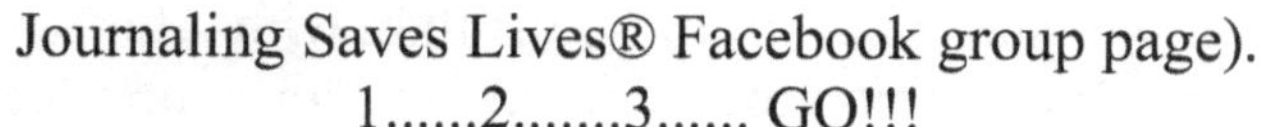

Journaling Saves Lives® Facebook group page).
1......2.......3...... GO!!!

Challenge: "If you love me then you'll do this or that" is a phrase that is often an indication of "Manipulation" which is proof that a person's SOUL (mind, will, emotions) is out of balance. It places a burden on others to do what you want them to do because you want them to do it. Expectations are necessary in many cases, however, they can also be destructive. How? When people don't live up to those expectations, it can create the spirit of offense and contempt, which then weighs both parties down. Understand, manipulation is an enemy to ALL healthy relationships. If you find yourself manipulating others, it's time to do a self-analysis to see how you got to that point and what you must do to change. If you find yourself the victim of manipulation, it's time to do a self-analysis to see what caused you to be manipulated.

Meditation point (keep in mind): If you are not "Bound" then meditate on how you can help someone else "Break free." Remember, someone else's life depends on your intervention.

Name 2 points that impacted you the most from Day 5

____

____

Day 6 – **Stop the Bleeding**

Journaling Exercise #6 (morning):

Psalm 118:24 (NLT) "This is the day the Lord has made. We will rejoice and be glad in it."

What better way to start your morning off than with a time of prayer and meditation? During this time, write in your journal; release ALL left over thoughts, emotions and ignored situations from the previous day. Never let yesterday poison today!

Challenge: Many people are "Bleeding" on everyone they encounter (family, friends, co-workers, strangers etc...) all because of unacknowledged and unresolved issues. Some people refuse to simply admit "I'M A TOTAL MESS!" If you are carrying "weight" because of past or present circumstances, then whatever good deeds and/or words you are giving out has your "blood (pain/sorrow)" attached to it and you begin to pollute those you encounter.
Do yourself and others a favor get healed and made whole. If needed, schedule a session(s) with a mental health therapist or grief counselor in addition to prayer, journaling and every other healthy habit. It's okay to do so!

Meditation point (keep in mind): Sometimes we have to invest in others ... It's good to be proactive to ensure those you love also have the tools they need to be sound in their mind & emotions. Who will you invest in today?

Name 2 points that impacted you the most from Day 6

____

____

Day 7 – **Peer Pressure**

Journaling Exercise #7 (bedtime):

Psalm 139:23 (NKJV) "Search me, O God, and know my heart; try me, and know my anxieties."

What will you do with the fresh BLANK PAGES in your journal??? They are waiting for you to fill them with all of your internal troubles. Take 10-15 minutes (or more) starting NOW, to purge yourself of that negative energy accumulated from today! Always make it a point to positively invest in your mind and emotions.

Challenge: How many of us have found ourselves trapped in destructive situations due to allowing someone or something to pull us AWAY from truth into deception?! Should we blame others or accept responsibility? Often times you can't be free from something until you pinpoint exactly what led you into it. If you're in this situation, you must first identify WHO and/or WHAT is at the ROOT then take the proper steps to break free and STAY FREE.

Meditation point (keep in mind): "Unforgiveness is like drinking poison but expecting the other person to die." Sometimes you will HAVE TO release the offender(s) from your soul without ever receiving an apology from them, that's LIFE! Take charge of your life today, don't allow others to control you.

Name 2 points that impacted you the most from Day 7

____

____

Day 8 – **The Danger of Affirmation**

Journaling Exercise #8 (morning and bedtime):

1 Thessalonians 5:17 (KJV) "Pray without ceasing."
Journaling should be a companion of prayer and meditation; together, these elements can and will produce great results as it

relates to maintaining a proactive grip on your mental, emotional and spiritual health. Never separate them! Set aside 10-15 minutes (or more) to simply write uncensored (whatever comes to your mind).

Challenge: EVERY human needs "some" affirmation from other people (some more than others); however, when a person begins to build their life (connect their worth to) on receiving kind, encouraging or reassuring words from others, this is proof their soul (mind, will, emotions) is sick to some degree. It is dangerous because if one doesn't receive affirmation this will have a negative impact on their life; in some cases will lead to a depressive state. Does this describe you? Time to do a self-analysis to find out what contributes to you unhealthily desiring affirmation then formulate a plan to overcome it.

Meditation point (keep in mind): Yes we should help others in their time of need, however we should not become a "Garbage can" in which people consistently dump their baggage into us. This will lead to burn out. Set up healthy boundaries in which to hold people accountable for their own health in the midst of you helping them.

Name 2 points that impacted you the most from Day 8

____

____

Day 9 – **Return on Your Investment**

Journaling Exercise #9 (bedtime):

Psalm 118:17 (NKJV) "I shall not die, but live, and declare the works of the Lord."
The gift of sleeping and resting peacefully depends on your ability to release and/or manage anything that hinders you from doing so!

Invest 10-15 minutes (or more) in yourself by purge writing before hopping in the bed. Trust me, your life depends on it.

Challenge: If we're honest, some of the "weight of the world" we are dealing with from various situations and circumstances is because we're simply receiving back what we've put out at some point in time. The law of "sowing and reaping" is a biblical law that governs everyone, everywhere and can NEVER be broken. Some of the baggage (frustrations, fears, worries, anxieties etc…) that's attached to you can be eliminated from your life by simply treating others with kindness, consideration but most of all with love.

Meditation point (keep in mind): If someone reveals sensitive matters to you regarding their life, keep it in confidence rather than using it as a topic of discussion (gossip). Let your words bring LIFE not DEATH!

Name 2 points that impacted you the most from Day 9

Day 10 – **Time to Say Goodbye**

Journaling Exercise #10 (morning and bedtime):

Proverbs 4:7 (NLT) "Getting wisdom is the wisest thing you can do..."
You do not have to react like society expects, due to negative external events and circumstances. The woes of life will happen to us all; however, those who have healthy outlets such as Journals will respond to adversity in a more effective manner than those who choose to "Internalize." You don't have to be a victim of life! Do

yourself a favor, for the next 10-15 minutes (or more) write, write, and write!!!

Challenge: The strong idea in scripture (Mark 6:4) is that many people, in order to bloom, grow and expand they must often leave their place of comfort (home). Why? Because those who have always known you (family, friends and loved ones) have a tendency to limit and place stigmas on you. In addition, there's also a tendency to define your present state of being based on the person you were in times past! This creates frustration, confusion, rejection and negative isolation). To prevent wear and tear on your inner being, it may be necessary for you to pack up and leave. A fresh start awaits you.

Meditation point (keep in mind): Wisely pick and choose your battles. Failure to do so can lead to anger, rage and paranoia which is often extremely difficult to unravel from.
Remember, everything doesn't deserve your attention OR response.

Name 2 points that impacted you the most from Day 10

____

____

Day 11 – **Who You With?**

Journaling Exercise #11 (morning and bedtime):

John 8:36 (ESV) "So if the son sets you free, you will be free indeed."
Whether you're Christian, atheist or any religious background, whatever your ethnicity, MENTAL ILLNESS is real among all mankind and comes in various forms. Many of which can progress to advanced severity when left untreated. What are you doing to better

your situation? The worst thing you can do is internalize (hold things in). Grab yourself a journal; and for 10-15 minutes (or more) give those issues a place to live other than within your mind, heart, spirit and emotions.

Challenge: The inability to properly assess and utilize wisdom will often lead us to form alliances, friendships and relationships with those who don't have our best interest at heart. The end result, "Soul Baggage" (betrayal, heart break, abandonment and more) much of which could've been avoided had we not been naive. Take extra precautionary methods when connecting with others (whatever the situation is).

Meditation point (keep in mind): Proverbs 19:11(AMP) "Good sense and discretion make a man slow to anger and it is his honor and glory to overlook a transgression or an offense (without seeking revenge or harboring resentment)." As the scripture mentions, learn to simply overlook things (sometime) without stress. Once again, everything doesn't deserve your attention!

Name 2 points that impacted you the most from Day 11

Journaling Testimonials

 **Allisyn Marountas** keep talking about it Bud..Writing got me through some of the worst times in my life. i was able to use the process to unload all of the sadness, anger, and frustration i was feeling and work through those emotions as well..it works and people don't typically think about doing it until they are in a place where they need to unload ♥

Love · Reply · 5d  1

 **Gina Cleveland** .....helps me fall asleep faster and easier; no continuous thoughts running around my mind

Love · Reply · Message · 8w  1

 **Glenn Payne** I beat the heck out of it...venting and its awesome feeling to do it.

Love · Reply · Message · 5w  1

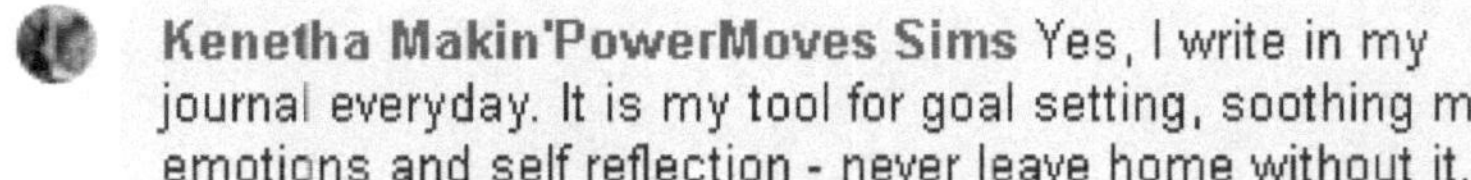 **Kenetha Makin'PowerMoves Sims** Yes, I write in my journal everyday. It is my tool for goal setting, soothing my emotions and self reflection - never leave home without it.

Love · Reply · Message · 2w  1

 **Mary Figures** Journaling saved me  1

Like · Reply · Message · 4d

The END!

Now that you've begun cultivating healthy mental, emotional and spiritual habits you must now "maintain" those same habits. This book was meant to set you on the right course now it's your job to find that "inner strength" to stay there.

If you need help and/or resources as it relates to your mental, emotional and spiritual health please email: <u>JournalingSavesLives@Yahoo.com</u>

JournalingSavesLives®

FREE JOURNALING
SPACE

FREE JOURNALING SPACE

FREE JOURNALING
SPACE